The Café at Light

The Café at Light

Mark McMorris

Roof Books
New York

ISBN: 0-931824-11-8

Library of Congress Catalog Card No.: 2004092270

Cover: *The Café Terrace, at Arles at Night* by Vincent Van Gogh

Acknowledgments

Sections of this book, sometimes revised, have appeared in the following peri-odicals (with thanks to the editors): "Black Pieces I" & "Black Pieces III (The Horses of Plato & Achilles)" in issues of *Hambone*; "Spring Journal" (selec-tions) in *New American Writing*; "Dialegomai (Suite)" in *apex of the M*; "Au Café Noir" in *Chelsea; &* "Figures for a Hypothesis," part 1, in *o.blek*. Other sections have appeared in limited edition pamphlets: *Figures for a Hypothesis* (Leave Books) and *Moth-Wings* (Burning Deck Press). "Black Pieces I" has been anthologized in *Ancestral House: The Black Short Story in the Americas and Europe* (Westview Press); *Moth-Wings*, "Panel One: Advent of the Hill," "Panel Seven: Notes for a Book about Danielle," & "Panel Eight: Interlude" in *An Anthology of New (American) Poets* (Talisman House); and "Flood," from "Black Pieces I," in *The Gertrude Stein Awards in Innovative American Poetry*, 1994-1995 (Sun & Moon).

Thanks to Beth Anderson, David Kadlec, George O'Brien, Jared Green, & Kim Coles. Nadia Sahely read the book in ms. too many times to count, and her sup-port was invaluable & unstinting.

Roof Books are distributed by Small Press Distribution

1341 Seventh Avenue, Berkeley, CA 94710-1403

Phone orders: 800-869-7553 **www.spdbooks.org**

 This book was made possible, in part, with public funds from the New York State Council on the Arts, a state agency.

NYSCA

ROOF BOOKS are published by Segue Foundation

303 East 8th Street, New York, NY 10009

www.roofbooks.com

For Sara O'Malley

Forsan et haec olim meminisse iuvabit.

Contents

I. Flood

    Black Pieces I   *13*
    Dialegomai (Suite)   *22*
    Spring Journal   *29*
    Black Pieces II   *32*
    Spring Journal   *40*

II. Dialogues in the Café at Light

    Figures for a Hypothesis (Suite)   *47*

III. The Sun Where Water Used to Lie

    Spring Journal   *69*
    Black Pieces III
      (The Horses of Plato & Achilles)   *70*
    Moth-Wings, or Panels of the Dust   *82*
    Morningside Memoirs   *102*
    Spring Journal   *104*
    Au Café Noir   *107*

Observe
the sun, warm
        and luminous in every direction
and the immortal bodies drenched
        in its violet radiance.

                    —*Herakleitos*

The struggle of the fly in marmalade.

                    —*W.B. Yeats*

I

Flood

~ Black Pieces I

Flood

Clearer now, in this state of darkness, the several pieces in one, that across the intervening years, I owe to each what I have become. There is no news of the self. In the power station, huge turbines sit silent as the water drips. In my name, St. John, the lights have been put out. The island lies reft of gladness, sodden the roots of crotons, gardens awash in rivers of stalk, petal, and wrack. The flood never ceases. At Queen's Street, at Matilda's Corner, along the Old Hope Road, a trickle of hand carts: a kettle, a photograph of Christ, a broadnosed ax, a lignum vitae bed, a cotton smock, a chest of drawers, an old man's hat, a grand-mother's clock, a mermaid of glass, a pair of workboots. The questions fall, they fizzle and go out. Parliament deserted, water babbles in the aisle, left bench and right bench empty of thunder. The empty seats, *e pluribus unum*, a curse. Women flee to the airport; a child stops, drinks from the puddle left by a donkey's hoof. No planes will kiss the sky, no bird will carry them to land. We are stuck, like a tree, I shout. Shade of Denzil, shade of Tanya and Charles, and the blank shadow of myself. We dance like the fates. Time passes, and clouds gather, and skies leak. Why not go in? A merciless whip, the lash of rain on my back. Where is the nurse, Martha the *angellos*? Her insides are bitter. Will she be appeased? Who can read this riddle for us? What man is not a riddle to himself? Do we aim too high? Why is the wrath unleashed? Why shall I die and not live? Why shall my race be extinct? Why shall I eat dust? Why go on my belly like a dog? Why do I stare at a blizzard? Why do I scratch at my face? Why do I shriek at Danielle? Why do I hate what I love? The stones talk only to plan our death. Day in day out, the workmen hammer nails, fit joints, saw wood, talk with a loud scrape, and they sing. Chisel and lathe sing to us asleep, doing our tasks, making love, eating soup, waiting for the day of god. Thus we are children to the last. We hunt pigeons by guile and set them loose. We wait for our flight. An old woman thumps her chest and looks grim. Her room smells of lilac or death. Charles has trouble breathing. He'll have to wait for the next bell. Danielle grows thin, stalk of celery. She'll have to wait. She will not again be the girl who followed me home. The next world, where is it? A long time in the oven. Earth is behind us; it rode upon the flood and sank before the flood. No land. Bah! "Let it be done quickly!" "Not yet," the poet said. Once, the lichen clouds, great boulders in the sky, swept over Riverside Park. A morning of the trees, cool air, and pale blue light, she will come. Only let it stop. *Pax vobiscum sit, undique verba tamquam imbres in me decidunt. Heu! a a.* Creeping things take refuge in the house, ant with snake, centipede, galliwasp. Black men die and deepen at the roots of cotton. Shrieks of the cockfight spill from my eyes, mouth, nose. This could take some time, I murmur. Liver? OK. Heart? OK. Kidneys? OK. Lungs? OK. Everything in place and working round the clock. The old cock. What a sight! The bird of god caws for some more liver. It bites, it draws, it feeds. The body lies open to the heaven. Eye of a red lid. Sunlight, rain, envy, ash, madness, skin, fire, death. The inner body seeps and quails, quakes, collapses on itself, and the dam of acid bursts. Sabotage, and the bird jabs. Terror, and the frame cracks. Frenzy, and the red eye of the moon searches out the One; her blade lies on my neck. Stars falter. Black sky, grey dirty morning, scream and cower of afternoon, dial-tone months, rock of Sisyphus.

Aspects of Black

: 1

I make seats for the arena, and on them, the *raison* for the building, the target, the colors that distinguish its areas, the black men, the blue girls, the red boys, the green women, the arrows (stuck into them) which create the hubbub that you no doubt perceive. The letters of the alphabet decide to fight it out. There is A for Antoine, B for Basil, and C for Carol—the latter androgynous and confused. They face forward like buddhas in a museum; they sit like rocks, like lizards in the sun, and hold colloquy with their own desires. This is how the fight goes. They share one hat, and I feel that my time would be better spent among individuals, Denzil, my friend, or Charles, or alone. The colloquy peters out, and then they leave. Each takes a different hat from the one he came in with. Only then does it become clear that three hats cannot occur in this scheme. Only then does it become clear that the letters stand for pieces of the host, wafer-thin mutations put gently on my tongue by a man in black. Antoine, Basil, and Carol build a language for themselves and put a stop to the fight. Yes, for then I will be in remission; then I will have some peace.

: 2

We come to the intersection at Avenue de Clichy. The road is clear. We cross to the metro stop and go underground. I think of a crack in the river tunnel that widens out of sight. As our train dips to the river, the fissure opens to a gash, and waters flood the compartment where Danielle and I sit. Our names float in the wreckage. Beside our names float the extra yellow *billets* Danielle keeps for an emergency. They go to the mouth of the river and are lost. Afterwards, an exchange takes place:

"Where are we now?"
"Where we were then."
"Who sits beside you now?"
"Who wanted to sit with me."
"Am I the person beside you in the dream?"
"You were asleep."
"Who is Madame N?"
"She was my confidence."
"And who is Tanya?"
"She was my infancy."
"And who is Charles?"
"He is my comfort. He takes the seat next to me."
"And who am I?"
"You were my sin, my anger, and my collapse. Unknown to yourself."

. . . &

Dialogue stops. Dialogue begins.

A dash of color from the violets. Rough brick. Other shapes
come into view. (People must be nearby.)

A sparrow from the mist. Goes into the mist.

No place to stand; no base for the figure.

One thinks with the mouth. I see.

A butterfly, a bumblebee: Cannot settle into the shape that it had.

Shape of horror   an egg yolk   a body   what I fill.

Seed of perishing or self.

. . . &
"I am black, like night," I said.
"All the threads enter and lose heart.
They thicken, and drag me to nothing."

"Write on the surface," he said.
"And read yourself in the spaces below them."

"I am too young to read. Too old
to learn how to write, too shadowy
for any seed to sprout in me.

"I eat space like a fire eats paper.
I consume myself.
This is the nature of my ash."

Saturdays (Danielle)

". . . He just sat down beside me. I thought—I can't be bothered. He began to talk. Of course I didn't. You'd have to see him. We had coffee once or twice. O.K. When the weather's warmer. Yes. I put down the paper. I did. He said it was fine with him, he'd like to go out for coffee and talk. Central Park? OK. Because he looked interesting. People have these weird lives in their apartments and you don't know about them. I was curious. The things that you hear. Tanya told me of a guy who raised pit bulls inside his apartment over on Madison Avenue. He snuck them past the door man in his attaché case and when they were about a year old, he sold them for the extra income. His neighbors believed that he had the same dog for years. Tanya thought that he wanted to go to bed with her and was making up an amusing story about himself. He became very serious, and invited her over to see. The oldest trick in the book, I don't know why she went. Anyway, the guy opens the door and it hits her smack in the face, dogs everywhere—in the front closet, the bathroom, under the kitchen counter, and the smell! He worked for Dean Witter and did not need the money. "Good day Mr de Angelis," and Mr de Angelis would go home to his pit bulls and truck load of Alpo. It's strange how the weirdoes stick to us like glue. Thaddeus—yes. Don't be dumb. He was a fat motorman from Queens. He drove the subway for a living and went home to write his novel. No, he did not circle round for me in his train. We took the bus. About 35. Will you let me finish? I know, but it was in the day and he looked harmless. You can tell. He was wearing an orange jacket with pink stripes—it was his day off—and dark glasses on the #2 Express. No, I did not do it to spite you. Charles is different—we are friends. No. I told you no. I got tired of him and didn't call him back. You get tired of someone who needs you all the time. I mean—I'm not sure how to say this—when we went out he'd tell me things, but I kept thinking, This sure is weird, boy. He liked that I had been in France and wanted me to tell him about Paris. Martha? If I say anything about her you will be upset. It was before we were together, I didn't even know you then. Of course it is! You were Tanya's friend. I knew you through Tanya. I didn't know that you knew her until we had come back. I told you. No. Charles and I are friends. It's not the same. We get along when we are together. In Greece. We

19

were traveling and it, I can't talk about this, it doesn't really have to do with you. I won't talk about this anymore. You never even told me about her. You call me Martha and I don't say anything. You know how that feels? . . . "

(Atropos)

Danielle tosses the balloons from her seat. I sit beside the Indonesian tiger and bat them back at her. The balloons jostle one another; a few glide to the piano where Charles sits with his wine glass and legs crossed. One balloon goes from Danielle's hand to my hand to Charles' leg, and he kicks it. Suddenly it bursts. Danielle says, "Heavens!" (Danielle is the only person I know who says 'Heavens!') Charles opens another bottle of wine. Denzil comes in with Tanya, and the fun begins. Tanya puts on Trench Town Rock. We dance like the fates. But Atropos is quiet, and the threads that tie us to her spindle slacken and allow us to choose. We are almost free from character, in between the bars of music. We slip from the bars, into a meadow of wine and desire, Danielle, Charles, Tanya, me, and Denzil. The talking has stopped. Careful not to trample and destroy them, careful not to expel, before we have had our fill, Danielle's breath that makes them expand, we step among her balloons. "This will not come again." Tongue like a gargoyle's, Charles wags his head to the music. But the music has stopped, and he waves his body to the silence. Nimble, quivering, water—the soul has these properties. Shadow on the front half of his face: an aspect of black.

~ Dialegomai (Suite)

Something went on, and is trying to make its way out of the dark; I feel its movement.

It is light, but moving so slowly we will collapse from anticipation or rage before it reaches us. And what insolence to equal our snail's slide along the leaf vein, a poor glass of water indeed!

Then the men in sweaters and white hair (for all their I-am-a-natural-force confidence) do not escape the dark. The chalk, like the moon they study, makes notations from another source, and cannot supply energy out of itself.

They write in a dead alphabet—that of the Greeks—to embalm what the Hebrew resurrection left behind, earthbound as that race is. I mean our bodies, left to go their own way . . .

Two words, haywire, under the Eucalyptus trees, alive in the pace of a sandal, closing like the boy Keats, unfinished.

Masterless, but the bougainvillea votes in our behalf for some decisive flowering or did, when through cracks of the moon in the jalousie window I saw it move, somebody's shoulder, and grow strange again.

* * *

My marble at bottom cracks so severely that the traditional fetishes—a pay check, eroticism—lose their spice altogether. One goes through the humping motion in a sort of disbelief.

On what grounds, then, might we decide which of the newer kinds of fetish to rub?

Categories fall in once more.

A battle-line indistinguishable from chaos. A mapping of desire, a map. Something to travel over but without the ditches, or the wild game.

Cannot support the hole. My arms are tired. But it keeps crashing in.

An awareness of the splinters of our hearts . . .

Of the ruckus in the tide pool—not merely as goings-on—but as what there is to it. What else would there be?

And the blind eye! How the beast howled!

An abode of microscopic animals all of them with ears standing straight up, attuned to a disorder we dismiss as their friendliness.

But it crashes in. Blew him right back to the island. And the winds deserted him.

You think of the body as the nervous tail of a lizard no longer on its baking stone, when in fact it is so much more. The tail is still palpable inside the brain, attached, waving as we speak.

And you are divided between them, like the joint of a finger unable to bend yourself, but at the crux of it: the wobbly pivot of Archimedes.

.

One observes the ambiguous cavities in the body as one observes certain kinds of exotic fish in a tank: from boredom.

Somebody, hopefully, will overfeed them.

I have bought a scoop net and practice on the tide-pool with the debris there, some of which I seal off, some of which I send to Danielle. She does not reply, but neither does she dis-agree, I'm sure, with my intention to drain the pool and fill it with fresh noise.

* * *

Think of Being as a door knob—but think, first, around language: you are bound to find a dog there waiting to jump all over you. It already wags a hard tail and . . .

Look, its footprints! I smell it; the hairs on my neck stand up tentatively.

An alibi, that's all . . .

Ah, there is the dog now. You are surprised to see how friendly it is?

A phantom. One cannot help but hanker after . . .

All the howls have been howled, and yet I suspect that we are still here. Do you agree with this? And if so, we are obliged to marry—correct?

Are we waiting? Do we sink? Up to our necks? Over?
On, Winnie . . .

"Footprints, as we see them erased, also cancel out the beach . . . "

Well and good!

Because yesterday, while you were mixing the lemonade, I thought: I don't think the world exists. But there I was all the while thinking it, smiling at the songbird, as if at a private joke badly told.

* * *

Fire   Part of a flame closest to the nozzle

Rose   A vase falling in silence, commotion of deep waters

Mask   Grimace somewhat misunderstood

Sparrow   Flutter over them, a minute glitter

Shell   Texture of missing, what the fingers turn up

Sycamore   Girl in green head wrap, at the stone basin

Vase   Black athletes black horses, an ideal place for a rose

Water   Turbid, pellucid, undertow, white: over a bed of
          gray pebbles

Music   Any dog's howl may be music

Man   A peep from the author's mouse hole

Cistern   A basket of simples cut from my weedy heart

Geometry   Pure rectangle giving rise to a jet of milk

Coffee cup   A black well like a rose

Domino   White eye, a Cyclops killing sheep, at the cave
          mouth

Paint   What flakes from the marble Venus, her shawl of rock

Wind harp   Dangle of no use without wind

Melody   Clear water from her mouth to mine

Breath   Dear melody from his mouth to mine

Kiss   Face of a buttercup nestled in spring grass

Radiator   A deaf snake that chimes in among blue

* * *

Things keep interfering. Good.
The mind is dusted, the heart
emptied of agitation waits
on my signal: everything in order.

As wind boosts the natural gift
of feathers, making blue air light,
so language, doing the opposite,
boosts my natural indolence.

Things keep interfering. Too many
faces have gone down behind
the wallpaper, I cannot drowse.
The birds—thank god—lack memory.

Good. Despair relieves the itch
in an adjoining room, the boil
of must breaks down and drains
to nothing serious, humidity lifts.

Things keep interfering. A door
slams open; or a songbird draws
out tranquil evening toward magic.
Good. A telephone. The day's dust

settles into the old furniture
of null and counter-null.
An archaeologist scrawls his note,
then dissents, and keeps digging.

~ Spring Journal

It is spring. Contours of events—no detail anymore—alone tell that she and I took the cliff walk at Newport. Danielle, and Danielle. A roomful of oscilloscopes—one cannot play favorites with these things. The Poinciana drop red petals to the asphalt. That little girl, that bruised knee, that khaki shirt smelling of sweat. The lawn to be cut, and the clippings raked into a pile and carried to the open land. (Danielle is underfoot.) The cups turn brown at the soft edges.

And Charles, next to the blue curtains in Danielle's living room, gestures to make his point emphatic. A motorcycle padlocked to the fence above the trash dump. Danielle's brown quilt. A caryatid or vase. Impressions that lead us nowhere: so long ago. Thick fever grass hiding holes, tentacled vermin, sharp rusty sheet-iron, etc. Only then does thought of hazard reach up and pinch the nerves. A tangle of words, or coat hangers. Morning glories open up purple streaked with white: a drift of the observation post, back and forth.

Hibiscus plants shield the untended ground of the open land. The daughters had grown into women. But earlier they would come out to the fence at my scream, short brown hair on the youngest, a pale face, like her father the old Mr Levine, retired now dead, on the middle daughter. (Danielle allowed me to pull her closer.) The father wore field shorts and boots at the end of an old man's legs. A younger girl kissed me to feel her way. It was uncomfortable but she didn't sob. There was the gully, once edges had been defined: fluid passage distinct from stationary sides, child from dirty water below, here and now ramparts from a litter of chronology. She got fed up.

Words into the mouth piece. Static moment similar to alcohol running low and night stalling in the midst of a crowded party. Things that were said. The stones cut right through the piano room where we spent most of our time in the first few years. Then, out into Brooklyn (when Tanya moved from the West Side with her English husband) and into Manhattan when they took the Chelsea apartment. The stones come from behind and whenever one looks back, they cease. Fog. Caught in mid-reflection, at the crossing point, what else to look for. It could go in so many directions. The several features join up in the end. Do they now. At any given point, the story begins to wash down the culvert. At any given point, it scampers past zinc and bamboo shacks propped near to flood waters; these shacks do not survive the rainy season. Residents rebuild them from pieces of wood washed down the gully and deposited in the mud after the waters drain off. A roof beam, a plank with plank with plank, makes a door. Beyond any given door, the stucco homes begin again until the residential district runs into the common open land of the Common; and after, the road rises or has been rising all along, for to the left is the deep valley of the Yallas River.

Unless one knows of it beforehand, Escarpment Road, half naked youths chase dogs, one another, matchbox houses of the village inside the fold of the Warika Hills. Someone comes to the gate. Younger brothers and sisters go to the shop for tins of condensed milk. The bar shouts reggae music at 1:30, the sun beats down and beats the asphalt and beats the weeds and dirt. Trees like orphans. Broken glass on the road or the sidewalk. Electric poles stand out in the sun-glare. Line joins line. Line joins house. The cars, some extravagant, balloon in the heat.

Elms glitter over here on the other side of the plate glass. The library cools down in the spring. The leaves have that iridescent green typical of April, as one goes back to the swirl of letters and book jackets for more news. A peach moment returns to a peach basket. Ostrich plume ginger, the sculpture garden at Devon House, a white colonial mansion by the stoplight, select their own stage and so compose whatever stage they see fit. One boy meets another in the housing development just outside Paris. Bicycles in tandem along the airport road wheel into the haze. The cool pebbles of the stream lie untouched. Not by chance did the children decide to pack up and go, but the photographs, which turned up in the move, make plain the ones who saw the sun rise at Papine. That was the starting point for all trips to Cockpit Country, Newcastle, Mavis Bank, Blue Mountain Peak, name it. Knapsacks of chicken and corned beef sandwiches. The girls, because no hike can prosper without them, not in uniforms but in frocks, like the foliage. Up on the trail, we veer off to a knoll and sit for a while and sun breaks in on us. The valley spreads out below. Then back into the rooms.

~ Black Pieces II

(Garage)

I was once more in the garage where she works
to elude the noise, in the blue shirt, with hair that sometimes
falls over her face, and is put back, a little wet. So much
to cherish as the wheel rotates, to stand back from
in shadow, among the hose coils, of her effort.
Burlap in dim light, the broken light of *Le Sud*. Plain
that I do not know anything about this woman. I know
that she waits for me to leave so she can contact a self
owed to the laws of angular momentum, the rush of
stillness as a body spins faster, and thoughts calm. The wet dirt
moves around, spinning, and becomes a vase, the shape of it, a neck—
a tapering neck comes out of her hands that press
and flares off at the mouth, one trick of the senses.

Nothing is finished in the effort to manage the liquid forms
that play around her absence from my touch, in this space
the words are much too loud for the task, like a noise of
baling and loosening that startles her then, until I leave.

Who shivers in the wind?
What broke our back?
Who ravaged the kiss?
Who dug up the seedling?
Who started the counterfeit?
—Hesperus falling. Hesperus as she sinks
and fades out to black.

(Travel)

Danielle wraps the cheese in cellophane and puts it into her knapsack beside the knife and paper plates. The Swedes across from us flip through magazines; after introductions, pleased that we too are students (we are not), they lapse into travelers' boredom and say nothing. Mercifully, there are only four of us in the compartment. The wine makes us dull, and we cannot get mush of anything across. Danielle says: "It seems that we have been on trains like this one ever since time began. Sticky vinyl seats in small cubicles, sticky utensils and wilted Camembert on stiff bread—soon I will be too old for this, the uncomfortable beds, the travel late at night." She settles the knapsack onto the floor behind her legs, and puts both of them up. "It won't be enough," she says, "a month is too short. You can't settle properly into your life." The wheels tell of our frustration, over and over, the same landscape from the window of a compartment on the cheap locomotive.

I have to get out of the heat—the heat makes me restless—and so with a small gesture to Danielle, I fumble through the door, and close it quietly, and go into the aisle. This is my spot late at night. I pull down a window and air comes in, it's louder than ever, out here: monotony. The night flashes past, ridge-lines in silhouette, the occasional fence-post and shrub, bordering the train tracks. From time to time, a glimpse of deep fields stretching to the horizon. The moon is resplendent, in a rock garden of clouds. I light up another cigarette. With Danielle asleep on the other side of the aisle.

What

cracked our pattern
ah! broke our backs
dug up the hibiscus plant
shivered in the wind
loosed our joints
cut short our fun?
—Woman on a bed of straw.
Birth. No sign of Love. Death
on extended wing.

(Manhattan Exchange)

The horse has given up the chase, and the wagon is tilting, and we're now at risk of toppling out. So close to the top. Up here, beyond the studs of Orion's belt, I was expecting to see Danielle holding the sable neck of a deer in her lap, and all around her in the black heaven, other signs of desire, her desire for me. I put the pennies and dimes casually on her shelf above the fireplace—unused—and take a seat on the wicker sofa. Danielle sits half-asleep by the television—mouth half-open—listing towards the window like a horse about to curve from the target, so close to the top. The air sparkles with notes from her flute, other notes from Martha's debut at the Conservatory. The cello in sunlight, on that afternoon, here in the living room with Danielle and myself, old news that won't retire to the archives. (Why is Martha, news of Martha, here with us now?)

Danielle under the nightlamp asleep. "Which one of us is the good horse, the horse that loves to eat apples from the charioteer's bucket—some of them are not even ripe—?" she asks. "I know you think that I'm the one that falters and drags us back to the body's confusion, but I don't think so. Are you sure?" I have never claimed to have this power for a fact. It was something I assumed.

One of the horses is the good horse and one is defective, like a tone-deaf philosopher who hears the song of a Naiad and changes the station on the radio. So close to the top. And when the last scholar hangs up the reins or goes mad—what of the team whose training is to rupture the heaven with a kick in the forelegs, to see the absolute form of the good, the face of a tarantula, a garden?

Danielle starts up from her seat, somewhat awake and unresponsive. So much has happened to us that there's a fragility to the simplest sentence. "O, so you're back," she says. "What do you want to do for dinner," she inquires after a pause. "I'm so hungry that I could eat a stallion. Are you my stallion?" Then she looks over at herself, and at me looking at her in the mirror above the mantelpiece. She is not entirely awake, as it turns out. Not immune to the promise of riding with the television on low, out to the pond that Madame N stocks with bass and keeps as a habitat for ducks and geese, in their long migrations.

Wind-harp

.

wind
(tether)

seedling

_____

Who broke our tether
Shivered the seedling
Damaged the light?

(Aix)

"We often hugged and kissed, Madame N and the girls. But there was one time, in the tulip beds and near to the azaleas, when I held on tight. I will never forget that day. The bones that jutted through the back of her blouse. The lilac water on her neck, her face powered until it was almost the color of chalk. How old was Madame N? She could have been 30, she could have been 60. She was the most self-possessed woman I knew. A tall Scandinavian with a taste for scarves and artifacts from primitive—I mean, other—cultures: masks, pottery fragments, that sort of thing. She used to intone: *forsan et haec olim meminisse iuvabit*, and it became a sort of joke. Who knows what it meant?

"I was living with a man in Pigalle, and too bad for me—I became pregnant. I decided to have an abortion. It was the only decision I could make. So I went. The procedure did not go well and for a couple of weeks I was laid up in bed. Paul and Isabelle took care of me. Little by little I started to get better, and one day they took me to see Madame N, and we stayed with her for a while, almost the whole summer. We spent hours exploring the countryside. That's when we had our long talks, mostly about her time in North Africa. She had another life before we knew her. And that's how I felt about myself—that I had lived another life, maybe even two other lives, before coming to Paris. One day, as if trying to tell me something, Madame N hugged me in the garden near to the azaleas. The others were in the house and it was just the two of us. It was a bad period, and my life had not been pleasant. But at that moment I felt I was with my mother."

Petals in a bowl of water. We come up water-logged. Danielle offered stories from her past as if continuing a narrative begun long ago. They started, came into the open space between us like a centipede, and then they were gone. You can see the apparitions. The dark body itself: black, black, black. (The two of us.) A mutual violation, and so little to show for the bruises. Our cities are named: Ann-Arbor, Kingston, Aix-en-Provence, New York, and Paris. I am writing to you from such a city. I will write to you again. Sunlight in the basin, the fountain on the Cours Mirabeau, which we walked on together, during this time of our travels.

~ Spring Journal

Other than these connections, what is there to stand in? Periods of sun-
light and periods of free-wheeling talk. The silence of damp smoke and
the death of a sparrow. Crevices on the hillside. When the benches were
put in, the boys and girls had a place to collect in between classes or
after. Lining the school fence, the bougainvillea plants under pressure
from these hoards. Everything that one notices can fit into the lime tree
and each tree produces a bundle of others. The gymnasium, a cinder
block building with a smooth concrete floor that sent back the light.
Cities string along like light-globes at a barbeque. This, then that, then
this, and nobody stays put. So-and-so unpacks crates and gets paid in
discount books. So-and-so joined the Peace Corps. So it is.

The front yard had a guinep tree, sturdy, tempting, restful and prosaic.
The guinep is a common fruit like an egg with green skin, but smaller,
about the size of a thumb. Danielle comes into the photograph that
leaves her behind, outside the white borders, like a misplaced glove.
Both escape the field of vision. Danielle returns to the yard after her
shower, wet as a porpoise, and she shouts: "You are idlers, and your
hands are empty nests." The crab-grass underfoot stays cool during the
summer. The house at Conolley Avenue stays cool as well. Curtains
drawn. Sun-shadow over yellow tiles.

The gully, once edges had been defined: a fluid passage for debris. Pasta
spills onto the stove. Over her shoulder the water boils. Lettuce, cucum-
ber, oil, carrot cubes, flop into the aluminum salad bowl. That her hand
scrapes them from the cutting board means nothing. Of course the
impulse did it. One evening from the pack. All evenings co-exist. No

40

evening remains. The evening can have a dozen shapes to it, ways of scripting, letters. Locate the real kiss. Part of my room, since I have composed it and am, keeps intact the Renaissance painting. But never the same one.

On our way out of Aix, Danielle had no qualms about tossing our keys through the mail-slot. No matter. Unless a failed modus operandi, unlike a marriage, retains its vigor till death do us part, that is. Two events collapse, she and me. The sparrow out in the storm. And the next day, after the barbeque, a difficulty to stop thinking erotic thoughts, despite her reply.

II

Dialogues in the Café at Light

Look: in my hand there's only an earthenware bowl.
                    —*Osip Mandelshtam*

It is a place.
Nothing has entered it.
Nothing has left it.
People are born

From those who are there.

                    —*George Oppen*

~ Figures for a Hypothesis (Suite)

for Danielle the interlocutor

Preface

I have been careful to put everything
from the walls and move the carpet
to one side, careful to avoid images
seen around the house and memorized—
paragraphs in the shapes of birds,
eye-shadows and women, glossy breasts.

.   .   .   .

How to forget the men who run ditches
for irrigation, and the women who sew
the fading tapestry that holds them—
who take thread from their own bodies,
pull apart the men digging the canal
to sew again their identical selves?
Those ditches will never carry water.
Love it is makes them repeat the task
but instead of talking we watch them.

.   .   .   .

All events begin to seem inevitable
when told repeatedly, in different words.
Speech does not invent but renews
the figure, and that intrinsic weave
is one fundamental of love. Poetry

likewise depends on some repetition—
of form and recital—to be at full value.

.   .   .   .

But to pick our way back into the cell
we condemn spools we have no hand in,
leave artifacts, and credit the dialogue
that we alone invent and take life from—
and make not a self but a plastic medium
and the austere lovers that we repeat.

Part I

1.

How far did we travel?

Till heart dried up.

Where did we start from?

A plan.

Where are we now?

Morningside. Aix. Mona.

What can words do that we haven't done?

Make a place. Then we can stop.

What is this place, if not a place to stop?

The yard is a loom; we begin with it.

To return? To begin again?

The model makes room for a setting out.

Why did we set out?

To get to a dialect.

Will there be one?

We know, after going through it, that there is.

Who else comes with us?

The yard is common: slave, poet, black.

And things? Do things go with us?

Bowl, fountain, vase, bird call, mirror, pigeon, cello, gravel, bed.

How did we choose what to take?

The yard gave them when we set out.

And people?

There are two of us on the trip.

Who is the slave?

A poet.

Who is the poet?

A black.

Who is the black?

A Greek. A nude athlete. A vase.

Is there a boy?

A boy left.

A girl?

There are two girls on the trip.
Do they speak?
No.
Who speaks?
Things. The yard. We speak for them. We recall what was said.
Where do things come from?
We make them.
And the materials?
We find them. The yard gives them. We assemble what we have.
And the plan?
Afterwards; we improvised it. We follow it.
What do we do next?
Stop. Make our way to the yard.
To make a hypothesis?

To see what we have left. What uncovered. What dissolved.
What muted. What dried up. What eloquent or emphatic.
What blooms. What wanes. What joins us to the yard.

The courtyard is what we missed.
The courtyard is what we have left.

We see it. There are two of us. A ring of houses, the common
    basin.
We speak about the basin.
We stand in it.
We fashion it: satyr, brooch, woodnymph, cello.
We find them.
We become white, hollow, and imperceptible. Things like a
    sound on the pavingstones.

2.

Water stamps its feet. Slant of rain, moss. What is this place?

The eye takes what it can use: panels of different lengths, some
empty, some littered with broken locomotive shafts, some
turned rigid—from such debris will the figures come up to light.

How far did we travel, to find our hearts waning but no rec-
ollection of having set out, although the model makes room
for it? Whom did we leave to show us, when we return, that
we have returned?

Not that far, and no one. We stayed nearby the hand making
these forms from us—to relate the dialogue clearly, woven out
of the yard.

And we arrived, then, after the incision?

Or after, when the heart, done with beating, undressed in
plain view and—poof!, disappeared, leaving this fountain in its
place.

How did we notice this vanishing if, as an inward speech, we
are its echo?

The yard is a loom of echoes. Hill versus cone, sphere versus
pebble: such distinctions do not bear on our loss. We draw
from the yard what we put back in.

And the quartet will come tonight?

That is certain. But after, residents of the townhouses will also
come to the balconies. They look down on the reviving foun-
tain as if to nurse it back, whatever caused it to diminish.

3.

It is night. The waiters pack up the tables and hurry home, so
that the musicians, who also wear black vests, may come in.
The four of them—one a woman —arrange themselves into a
bow, sheet music and stands in front of each chair. They
express docility, and do not prefigure excitement, in the way
that a boxer does.

We are not of the place? (Sight-seers like birds out of a cage.)

Spectators trickle in and soon overflow onto the sidewalk
opposite. Around us, the houses with their common basin
seem to drain our shadows into contours of the basin. And
these contours, which come to life in several competing
strings, the moon puts into relief. We become more white,
more hollow, more imperceptible, as if a sound lay upon the
pavingstones.

We left Marseilles? How long have we been here? It is already
dark.

The fountain and the music do not run simultaneously. The
one is doused while the other, like fragmentary light, plays on
the townhouses. The cellist looks at the frieze, at the battle of
Titans on one end, at Apollo on the other, at her place in it,
at ours, next to the water-carrier. The bow sings. The point of
the cello seems to drill the pavingstones until the first violin
takes over. Schubert in Aix. Avignon is next door, the Popes.
South and across, the border with Italy. A truck parked down
the street brings necessary incongruity to the picture. Satyrs
on jugs, satyrs on chairs, woodnymphs, are in the frieze but at
a level of detail too fine for the naked eye.

Bulls on the shutters. What are we looking for? The thing
missing.

The evening winds down. The spectators have gone home. The cellist has taken up her seat and gone home. A residue of music stays with the audience until the next concert. This is what we perceive in coming to the yard. Although it is late, that sound trickles around us and inhabits the blank panel on the frieze. It has several memories—but we know it as amber-colored light: street lamps when they are lit. The cello itself we remember from pictures of lute players, poems about citharai that the Greeks used, wind chimes in British gardens.

There has been an aftermath.

The woman has her own place on the frieze apart from her place as the musician in these figures. She is the water-carrier in one panel, the caryatid in another. Her language is the language of clay vases that turn up in the dung-heap, with laundry lists, brooches, household expenses, sometimes a few lines from Archilochos. Lovers turn up, preserved by the desert. Names turn up. This is the yard as we come to inhabit it.

As if the moon lay cloth upon a stone basin . . .

A moon, a tabac and café, the fountain of course, water-babies reclining as if upon a jet of milk, vapour. The caryatids kiss although on opposite sides of the room. They kiss by memory of people who kissed under them. The model makes room for a setting out.

As if, in a locomotive from Marseilles, the moon kept pace with our cab, always peering, always searching out some meaning of the dialogue, while we slept.

The house is old. With it, one inherits an expanding vapor, the way loss thins out whenever more rooms are opened. Some of them, with southern exposure, some in sleep always, their faces turned inward like a row of pigeons: but all crowd the fountain at night, and we cannot escape them, once here.

Congress of lively detail, black railings from the balconies overhead, a fine gold skin: this is our first setting, among auditors, more than a hummingbird's flutter, more than residue.

We inhabit the yard, after the cellist takes up her seat and goes home. We listen to her music trickling around us: not distinguished from amber-colored light, but this is our wish, not possible.

We condense as water that flows together out of air, ash.

Part II

4.

Dialogue precipitates in the space left by the music, formed out of nothing and filling it. Under the willows is a stone bench that lovers use. They walk to it and sit on it and hold hands. The moon dies. Only the voices of wind and fountain, syllables in the basin, come from the yard. The walls move in closer; the fourth side, formerly open, closes to complete the shape: a cube with no roof, tar above it.

Who is touched to life first? By whom?

We find it impossible to touch under the cross-hairs of a microscope. Look more closely: no one touches. Instead, we ward each other off, two antiphonal words that cancel, loss that, though multiplied, doesn't cease.

Another figure: that of a single fabric keeping us (them) hemmed in. Orphaned to these phrases and we cannot leave.

Conversely, wholly unimaginable, except as confused voices, a mob during the Revolution, say.

Frightened, in either case, by so many glances in so extensive a foyer, the nth mirror.

A yard-sale already concluded, but still announced daily.

Perhaps we cannot hear what it is we inhabit: water.

Each time I turn on the radio, I listen for a change in intonation, a stress on the Viennese lampshade or on the ceramic things. The pavingstones will not budge, nor the weeds that harp on them and cling, stronger than cement.

And, if it should rain?

If it should rain, then, and only then, do we transfer the table to St. Paul's vestibule and put out the books, the spoons you once thought were artifacts, the cigarette box, the intaglios of missing.

And someone will turn these things over, as they say, with loving fingers. Because they are purchasable.

We touch so invisibly that only mathematics can part the intervals, descending, as the fountain descends to zero, to one. And this is the kiss of the caryatids.

5.

One cannot walk to the edge of the yard. In spray from the
fountain, nothing is also in between droplets, just as wet,
though admittedly more vaporous than we seem.

And, as in the electrical field, which is at all points a field, or
which is at no point a field—for one part of the yard to cease
all of it would have to cease. I cannot survive our separation,
you know that. I,

A drinking glass, then
a drinking glass with intellect—on its coaster—
         a light rattling inside the glass, in air
Death of the glass—as if it vanished
         and left no trace of itself, no glass powder
         no ash of glass

And all drinking from glasses would cease. And the table. And
we who sat around it. And what we'd hoped the glass held
when you bent your lips toward it—how I held my breath like
a butterfly on a pond, then—a moot point.

And we see one another around the surface of the glass and
on the other side touch, hands. This is a feeling we have and
it has been confirmed independently, or soon will be.

Water vapor is not held by the hand. It is left to wander with
no force of gravity to plant its feet firmly. It floats at angles to
the surface or upside down, tilted as in the Marc Chagall, but
not so well dressed.

And in holding your hand body returns to it and gravity
begins to operate. That is why, against your wish, I held on to
your hand.

Certain phrases take their roost in the heart and come to stand for it. These, you may read.

But I already murmur them and you already kiss me to repeat the syllables: in this way I might take shape from you.

Kiss me to listen closely to what the heart says in that space.

To listen, as the poet says, and encounter in that hallway . . . not a ring of dancing peasants.

Certain cadences . . . at the periphery of speech, a cooing.

A dialect forming at the edge of the yard where drain pipes scamper under the walls, into dim avenues.

Where the silence is, not where the confusion is. Confusion belongs to the weeds under our feet.

Silence, because no one comes back from the avenues, and our water was last seen drifting towards this limit—deafened by silence.

.

Phrases that move out into sentences begin as ground for declaration, but then relinquish it. They want profundity.

The ground on which we must begin. But this is only temporary—a provisional flatness so that a whole yard can be built and once there, dispensed with.

As if the mirage waited until our lips had already kissed and then, when hunger began, showed itself as such: we are invited to pass into the dark of one another by this ruse.

And we must swap eyes, and look off into the retinas. For it is there that what the woman sews becomes our rendezvous.

One has her knitted shadows past all confusion in the sycamore. I will wait for you—but hurry!

To be in silence where birds gather like words on a cistern. So that you may listen to them. So that we may hold hands among them. So that our hearts hold.

Part III

6.

*The walls have closed to complete the shape of the dialogue, and
the frieze surrounds and contains them, birds out of a cage, at
the entryway to the dark. Among the nearby objects is one that
provokes the exclamation: "Look: in my hand there's only an
earthenware bowl!"*

*Otherwise, the yard is quiet. Symmetry moves among the objects,
among the nearby athletes, on the faces of the vase.*

*A symmetry without duplication of the mirage—the vase caught
up in a life of reflecting surfaces—the voices of the self built into
the courtyard, as permeable border.*

.   .   .   .

*They taste each other in a mirror; they lie in a tangle, like coat
hangers on the floor of a closet.*

The tangle of their voices touching one another in a word.

*They kiss in shadow of the caryatids around the perimeter of the
yard, the white basin.*

*She peels an orange at the table and shadows disappear. The vase
sits close to her hand—in the yard—the fountain shoots up into
sunlight. The water runs—mysterious and fluid—under the
yard, between the tangles, the roots.*

Water at the roots of an olive tree: core of the self.

*And there are two mirrors, one rose vase the same for each, one
broken vase that spills the irises, one woman in the yard, the cellist:*

The bowl is the shadow of a bowl
The cello is the hand of her shadow in water
The strings are its roots
Water is a cistern composed of our words
We sit on the cistern in sunlight
To read letters of what lies outside the yard
The tables are arranged for lunch
Waiters in black vests put vases on them
For us
        and we take two chairs under Van Gogh's cypress
And one of us says: *Le Bureau de Change.*

It is a sparkling day in Provence;
the blue sky, which we elsewhere call heaven,
floods the eyes like an unbelievable sea.
The water babies belong to the fountain
under the moon, one of the nighttime yards,
and have not yet come into view—
and so we observe the clock tower,
Hôtel de Ville and stop at the fromagerie
to look at the goat cheese, the cream.
I go on to the library, you to the studio
in the carriage house to make ceramic things
cup and saucer, ewer, clay
in turquoise, daubed with black spots—
and I hear the wheel turning
the forms soon ready for the oven
then a glaze to coat them—rust, green, peach—
they hold water then, and I still have the one you gave me
on the desk, in front of me, full of pennies,
full of kisses even so long after.

Our life has lost its symmetry, but we shape
each other somewhat more at night
as, more surreptitiously, the yard glimmers
open from a bedroom window,

and a big-lunged baby howls across the alley
like a jagged nerve.
                         To which you light a candle
and I pour more wine and cut the cheese; ·
we dine, this is what we do together
as a careful way of neutralizing time
until bed and sleep take us, and turn us in.
Rescued, we don more amicable masks
and slip from our usual clothes into the streets,
gardens, and desires typical of dreams
that stop short of morning. And so the night wanes.
And so much is forgotten, except the lines that tie us,
until a huge bomb in a nearby café goes off
and shock waves rattle the shelf and startle us.
Everybody gets out of bed, back to bed
through splinters on the sidewalk
and by three-thirty everything's quiet
as it was—but some are much wiser now.
Nothing in the paper about it—
a contemporary ruin: it's not our business;
it's the Arabs; it's another couple.

The skylight of Cezanne's studio
bids us enter—come, come—
to see the green bottles that held his candles
in fossilized charm, the wax
long ago dripped and hardened on them
or forms like the ones he knew
a skull, a letter desk, an easel
(to keep our hearts intact), bowls of clutter,
paint brushes, feathers, a jug,
cypresses from on high, not yet in the frame.
We bask in scattered relics of the art
on his spot, and think our way to forms
or windows that send us from the room
into a countryside of our choice.
This is Provence and not kingdom come

to earth, a yard and not our Purgatory
though the trees do look like fire—
though cinders menace, and we are not happy.

I remember you as a disturbing image
from the film of a *French Lieutenant's Woman*
or Ophelia, as she sang down the
stream of language and pulled the wildflowers to her.
That was her poetry
lost to both of us before the play began.
Your face terrified me—
turning at the sink, you screamed
and crumpled, unaware of me beside you
and singing like a madwoman
or a child and a broken doll
deserted on an island, unaware of me,
when you heard my voice you screamed
and crumpled, I could not
reach you then
               nor reach my self
after that. We'd come to the end of our travels.

7. (Afterfigure)

Depth had been taken from the yard prior to our arrival, and though from a different speech we could yet register this loss, an accretion of things misplaced or forgotten about. What drained from the walls and the eaves with each new family moving in, till the quiet moon ever more shifted and whitened the expressions from death to life, revived the figures on the ambient frieze of the yard? The eye takes from the speechless marble what it can of the stories carved on it; and uses this debris to fashion a place, void of noisy clutter, wide enough to stand in two abreast. There are a few blank panels, but most are thus littered: a broken locomotive shaft, split greaves made of bronze, a water jug, Pan at his rutting, sherds of ostraka, the callipagistic Atropos at her loom, embers from Iphigenia's pyre, timber from Odysseus' ship, and a rowlock. What we assemble must look like where we have been, in our moments of the interlude. Danielle still sleeps beside me and I too am asleep. The figurines and toys lie still on her shelves where I saw them, a red shower curtain keeps the light and serves as drapery for the windows of her bedroom. Close at hand, recrimination, pent-up violence, the ungoverned. Words can smash when they try to break out. And to speak from this place, to be within it, a temporary illusion of peace. The heart is gone out. This fountain that continually swoons—often plain with a plain cistern, often encrusted with water babies and pissing cupids—survives in its place, as words from courtyards that we visited. Then it too goes out, and what we know about each other comes back. Ghiberti's doors, which we touched, forever keep panels of the expulsion, or like a love cast in bronze, like a sword guarding the gate with fire, the language of exile accretes, figures for a hypothesis, on a panel not yet littered with our debris.

III

The Sun Where Water Used to Lie

The light of common day.
—*Wordsworth*

~ Spring Journal

The light persists, the noise persists, the isolated room where I sit writing these notes has an orange diffusion but whether of light or of sound—the distinction does not matter. Something ties me to these birds and to the life that they clamor about, in several tones, the different densities of chirping, from left and right. I stopped to listen to them, but how could I put a stop to restlessness as completely as their singing stops all questions of ontology?—part of an old discussion ("young men grappling with inexact terminology") that I used to have with Charles. The palpable sweetness, the confusion in the evening, my exhausting reflections on personality and on Danielle left me open to the music, but only to a point, only so far as I disappeared and entered, having been caught off guard. Now, trying to read in the after-wash of their discord, I am pulled back from the middle of the choir, and back from any tranquility that might have flowed from them. I am of two hearts about the songbirds: one is with them and of the same throat, the other makes notes quietly and listens, but listens too attentively to hear what the innocent hear, a glass oblivion.

~ Black Pieces III
(The Horses of Plato & Achilles)

You are free of death, you will not get old,
Yet ephemeral disasters torment you.
> —C. P. Cavafy ("The Horses of Achilles")

: 1

I've read the fable so often that it must be true, and if so, we are only distant pygmies, corrupt horses, earth-bound and broken-limbed. The charioteer—this figure stands for the intellect—guides his team towards a rendezvous with the *primum mobile*, the crankshaft that spindles through the mist of stars and anchors the geological core. The spindle turns. The chariot sweeps above the outermost rim of the universe—like the undecorated behind of a tapestry. Other horses stomp the battle-field. Words will not console or touch them. The poem about the hors-es that weep. What could we say to ameliorate their shock? Two teams of horses: one team pulls the soul outwards, the other team watches in disbelief and torment, the body of Patroklos beginning to smell under the Phrygian sun.

It's the middle of October and already cool in the evenings—a month, as Danielle says, when Philosophy asks the right questions. Fall is the time to listen to the dialogues of maple trees and the light. We are out on Broadway at the corner of 116th Street, offering each other the gift of consolation, the gift of speech: "There, there," we say. Syllables charged to deliver our wishes and assurances. Within the syllables that cross from one mouth into the cooling night, another image coalesces: a team of horses tapping the concrete to get our attention. "Our grief is undying," the animals whisper. "Please don't offer us your philosophy. Philosophy will not console us," they cry. "We want to change places with the team in the other fable, on their way to the empyrean."

I've read this fable before. I've read the fables so often in my sleep that confusion is my normal situation. How many teams of horses does Zeus stable on Olympus? Which team fights at Troy? Does the identical team take the soul to the circle beyond the planets? Was there a team standing on the Meadow when Diomedes—someone—chose rebirth as a weed, as a grasshopper? What could desire be, if not the body of an immortal horse watching Patroklos with a spear through his neck? Is there a language where the verb *to weep* and the noun *desire* share identical beds? I suppose, to my mind, that there must be, since I'm lying in bed with both the word and Danielle, and I am lying in the same bed as myself. Someone is weeping.

We are out on Broadway at the corner of 116th Street, in the October evening, with the Pakistani vendor standing in his kiosk, framed by chewing gum and cigarettes. I'm browsing the covers of glossy fashion magazines: skin exposed to the night. Soft allure. Object of sex. Danielle reads a *Village Voice* for movie listings, not speaking—not in bed with me under the red shower curtain, locking out the vapor and the night. Traffic passes behind us; people enter and leave the bookstore with packages. On other evenings we amuse ourselves with the fable of the team on its way to the spindle—or is it the body of Socrates, left to decompose at the city gates, for the crows to contemplate, that causes us to scream at each other like that?

"That's got nothing to do with me," Danielle says. "I can't believe you'd think of me as the lover of a dirty old man."

The horses paw the concrete. I watch them reflected in the plate glass of the bookstore: their frightening bodies, the black hair slicked down, the leathery sides, the power in their necks. War-horses to pull a chariot out of earth's orbit, hard against the winds of gravity. This is the meaning of the fable. The walls empty, or at best, a mirror where the figures used to hang. Two teams of horses, or the same team in both

71

fables. The imperfect soul is always subject to weight: the charioteer as the bulging form of the horses, asked to do more—more than he can.

(The horses are immortal. Patroklos is not. The Olympian god dismisses him as an "ephemeral disaster." That is the meaning of the fable.)

Danielle used ride in Central Park, especially in the early part of May, when the plants are still surprised by the heat and their own health. Tonight, she replaces the cover on a pot of simmering stew, and goes into the living room to finish the crossword puzzle. Lamps on low. Somehow a peace. I'm deep in the fable of the horses. In fact, the horses are at the living room window, and their weeping is like a dying locomotive. "Do not weep for us," I think. "We will weep for our own defective kind." What do the horses make of the stream of the dead, standing in the Meadow? What is the ratio of desire to the bone *études* of a piano? Who can trail her fingers like a waterfall to summon the executioner's death?

:2

This is a fable of our own defective kind—on certain summer evenings in Manhattan—

—a crystal wedge in the shape of a team of horses, to keep abstractions in the penitentiary where they rot—

—on certain summer evenings in Manhattan—

—a fracturing of light into spectra: red to violet, just as the horses initiate a prism to fracture and display the colors of desire—

—two horses on their way to the outermost rim of the universe—two horses are speaking—

—the planets revolve like bowling balls and emit the music heard in the poet's harp strings: *menin aede thea*—

—I have heard this music myself—I know the language—

—on certain summer evenings in Manhattan, when the night holds back her skirts on the far side of the river, and the big sun slows and hovers—

—on certain summer evenings in Manhattan—

I once believed in the story of the horses and the charioteer, because the red sun would not set, because the domino tiles would slap a table by the liquor store, because it seemed that, given a choice between this story and Scripture, we knew which had to be a metaphor, some words are like that, some words happen to you forever, and to hear or read them to yourself is to step sideways from the illusion of automobiles on Riverside Drive, and think:

"Nothing can stop these words. I've waited on them forever."

The night had no beginning, and leaves glittered overhead like spangles on a golden cuirass, and the river running. Patroklos lay dead on the meadow. Achilles was furious. The leaves trembled in the breeze. It was late at night, and Danielle and I, taking our customary stroll in the park, were stupefied to think that somewhere, on such a night as this, the armies were mustered for invasion, with the sharp swords waving.

—on certain summer evenings in Manhattan—

At every second, at every pause in the riot of scattering grief, a voice comes over the loudspeaker inside my head: it promises that help is on the way, help in shutting out the stars and excess water, help with the tangle of metaphysical systems that never grow real like an orange.

I am not convinced that this was long ago. On that particular night, I took hold of Danielle's arm to steady her walk, and we went by way of Grant's Tomb to the apartment and the warmth of the living room rug. We kissed each other on the chessboard pattern of the lobby. Intact, the ashtray and wine glasses waited on the moment they would topple and shatter, just as the spear head shatters when it meets the boss on a shield. The horses wept to see the hero felled by a system that crumbled at the moment most needed, and the soul shrank and went up in smoke, there on the shore with the ships drawn to landward, pointing their backs out to sea.

:3

Whenever it is raining and the liquid hyphens plummet to the steaming asphalt, the horses of Achilles are said to be weeping immortal tears for the corpse of Patroklos, dragged through the weeds and broken spear shafts.

Whenever it is raining fullstops and clauses, pronouns and verbs, in the steaming city by the Hudson, the horses of Plato have failed to cross the gates of gravity into the forms of pure ideation, beyond the titanium canal of the last planet: *planao*, to wander, unlike the earth which keeps still, like Odysseus before he read the 24 volumes of his wandering life and chose to reject it.

(The rain interrupts the battle. Incidentally, the rain douses the fire, and the fable's subject—Er—gets up from the charred wood of the bed. It is raining on the gunmetal ships on the western edge of Manhattan. Other islands are wholly invisible to radar. No matter. Someone at a blackboard is saying: The universe is like an orange in the upturned palm of a demon. The demon is altogether like a microbe on the tail of a sheep dog. And so on. The universe is like a sheet of yellow paper with no back. And yet, this should not be cause for alarm.)

Whenever it is raining and letters of the alphabet deluge the periphery of speech, the horses step forward. They whisper: "Our grief is undying." There is a flood, but no lightning or ferocity, a tranquil rise of water until the towers surrender and sink. The horses cry: "We blame ourselves!" Zeus says to himself: "I should not have been so rash as to give you to a mortal, even as a gift to Peleus who wed Thetis the sea-nymph, *athanatos*, on the slopes of Mt. Helicon or somewhere." Meanwhile, the other team gallops through asteroid and vacuum, and one of them balks—the wing goes lame—and flutters back to earth and misery. This is a story about the interrupted (f)light.

.

:4 (The Man from Signal)

We know the importance of signals that can travel large distances to contact the stewards of chance. And thus the man we call Morse, Denzil's name for him. We come in from the stoop to listen:

        tap   tap   tap   tap

A blind man walks with a cane in the airshaft. The night yawns. Orchids bloom in the whistle of tree frogs. Elsewhere.

        tap   tap   tap   tap

A weary code, a weary code. But the thumb cocks the hammer and the first digit curls around the trigger. The comma in the row of type. The mallet testing for the reflex. Here—no it is not there—it is over here, listen:

        tap   tap   tap   tap

The noises are not so regular. They have a mad logic of spacing and intensity, a combination of pitch and meter intended for a silent, recondite addressee somewhere beyond the visible.

The night is tiresome. Morse is restless, a cypher. I shout at the neighbors who shout back at us. A horse limping from battle, a girl cracking a boiled egg, a coal miner after the scaffold's collapse, a roof leaking into the sauce pan, a bathroom tap leaking, a carpenter putting up a portrait.

        tap   tap   tap   tap

We respond with serial bullets aimed at our neighbor: several erratic thuds, a few taps like glass breaking, soft taps like a centipede's legs on vellum, the thunk of a fist on the chest. Charles is very good at this game. So the summer night passes in communication between the two apartments.

*   *   *   *

This so-called Morse, who is he? We have met cyphers under the names of Antoine Basil Carol. Comes now a man who has no more substance than a method—a substitute for language. You might say that Morse, insofar as one may assign being to an empty space, resides in a comparison of durations. Long or short—determine only that, and there he prowls in his apartment with the World War II radio set. Morse is the imperceptible difference between two sounds. He exists only for the dog that he has not yet purchased. Only mathematics can chart his obsessions. He's waiting for the letter we all wait for on the upper west side.

:5 (Confession)

I am Morse, of course. I am, or will be, many people in my dream.

Antoine Basil Carol—three of the alphabet that I e-nounce to myself, or that says me to itself, when it wants.

Morse wrote yesterday: he's doing fine in Albany. Thank god he found a job at last.

Danielle has left me for Charles. There, I've said it. I imagine I'll get over it soon.

Dave Edgar Finnegan Garth Hengist Iphigenia Kwame Lot's wife Morse Nyabingi Ophelia Paul (St.) Quaestor Rambunctious Simon Peter Topic United Vermin Winded X Yusuf ibn Tashfun Zodiac Alphabet

:6

The morning is easier. Danielle is awake now too. Like the mountains or groundskeepers below, she's an activity to consider, and comes to sit with me out on the balcony. A mouthful of intersecting systems—the solitude of a meteor and its purpose to crash in a fireball, into the blue habitat of fish, or a comet violating order with order of its own, but it's daylight for at least 10,000 miles of the bulge, as the person walks. We're unable to think badly of the universe, in spite of proof. A bucket of clams hauled from the Caribbean Sea is also mysterious. How we met and how we attacked tore each other up. A story is in this too.

Danielle grows dim. The craggy boulevard with tenements given over to heroin addicts. A neighborhood that saw, in the hours before sun-up, the firebombing of entire blocks. The eye-holes with souls—blackened walls, dilapidation, on streets only a morning jog from Claremont Avenue. The others, farther in the north, where the elevated train supervises standing rubble. By fire or by flood. The body can break in two even as a person walks to the bodega.

Danielle grows dim, but the scorching of the boulevard continues and catches me off guard, only partially dressed. To be candid and even ridiculous, I cannot avoid the Greek words: *apothanein thelo*. The *o-mega* of diminished sigh. I speak them over and over. The extreme weather conditions want to have their day, never mind the activity of car wrecks, bodies in church doorways, women with arms like thighs, swollen and sore-riddled. The body sets small fires in oil drums. The horses whisper to each other—disgusted, their education complete.

Danielle and I are on the back slope of the park looking out at the Hudson. The day is chilly; wind troubles the river into white froth. We are amused. Without preamble, Danielle declares that she cannot understand the fascination with tight jeans. "I mean, why would you advertise your fat," she says. The traffic is light, only a bicycle, a stray taxi obviously with a driver new to the city. Or the day is stifling. Dirty as it is, the river flows on calmly. Danielle cannot understand the fascination with tight jeans. "When I was in Paris," she says, "Alan used to have these Americans to dinner. They all wore the most hideous clothes. I mean, why would you advertise your fat." I do not ask her about Madame N or the *oubliées*, the stray girls who were with her on the estate in Provence. That is another story for another situation: a book yet to be conceived, much less written, with other ephemeral characters.

:8

On those summer evenings in New York, before the hammering mania of total humidity smashed our converse, before it seemed possible to spend a day in the Cyclades, a night in John Keats's house, to ride on the flatbed of a lorry going in the vicinity of Marseilles, then Danielle and I would talk the length of the park from Grant's Tomb to the flower beds at 81st Street, and there was no end to the golden minute, which lasted as long as the poem invaded the syllables, the noises of salsa and carhorns, the cymbals of light crowding the belly of the river. It was poetry that made it exist.

~ Moth-Wings—
or Panels of the Dust

Vestibule

There is a fable of a haunting. The haunting of a man. Listen. As in another fable, a man slept until he became indistinguishable from the ground he slept on. The grass crept between his arms and sides, spread over his wrists, grew thick between his ears and his neck, and then the rains fell and watered them. Flowers began to sprout from his fingers. Hedges replaced his eyebrows. High over the hillside the guillotines circled. They studied the dreamer's face. Behind him in his sleep, the shadows were gathering. The small meadow or *saltus* expanded to enclose the form of a translation, the wooden platform before the cold tracks. A shrub sprouted from his abdomen. Three figures huddled at the edge of the platform. No train was due. Within the space of the dreamer, voices began their perorations, their interference and syncopation. The eyelids of the dreamer acquired the texture of tree bark. Three voices that belong to three figures. The letters of the alphabet. That was all. The seasons changed on the hillside. Armies fought on the plain below the hill. Their choreography swept over the hill and danced towards the cliffs. The dreamer slept on; he made a dream of the alphabet. He did not know what he was dreaming. A guillotine said: "I am by far the best at seeing small things from a great height. I am the telescope of god." And what did the guillotine see? He saw the alphabet in colloquy within the space of the dreamer. And what did the letters say in the dream? (This could be important.) Alas, the guillotine, sharpest-eyed of god's creatures, could not hear what was said. He circled above the man. But no words reached him—only the silence of the hillside. The rain swept over it like an army.

Panel One: Advent of the Hill

The word—the husk—splits open, and out crawl tiny black ants, each with a piece of the man. I am scattered among these ants; like them, I am become part of a trail that moves, joining the hill to the garden.

Left behind by the rain, a puddle in the dug-up earth. A dead moth in the puddle. What, I wonder to myself, will happen to this moth, the colors on its wing all bright in death?

.

When the sun sets, the leaves whirl in the yard with force, and the rustle is of feet in the wood, countless words. The whispering of faded detail. Faded people walking hand in hand, admiring the beauty of the wood, the naked branches overhead, like the wings. Faded words, and well used, taken up and turned over by the hand.

Out in front of me, a flickering moth still in sight of the orchestra, smaller than a blade of grass, of an earth color, mingling with scraps of rust. The iron wing-drift of the moth. The uncanny present of the moth, big with effort, dense.

The ants come to haul us to a section of the earth cone they use for debris. All the words are there, black and red, long words and lowly, foreign words and familiar, piled up in a heap—of unbleached rice. Dead ants next to the moth, which is dead, and the languages thin from overwork. We carry them to the foot of the hill. We come up from the cellar. The line from hole to hill, to dirty puddle with the moth, and back to the hole, the nest. I am at the outer part of the nest.

The hill is a vessel for the ants. Who will fill it once it empties for the night? The storm of ruin comes to our house. The storm of a common day. And the body lies broken on the hill, the weaver-woman spent, and the ants with rice in their jaws. The mirror lies face down, in the garden. The body in time, moving from grass to grass. I am with the ants, black among the red, no longer drinking from the light, no light leaves, all is black, for now. Or not even black, no more than common. The whole yard springs from the tree, the roots of the tree meeting in the trunk, and branching into sky and fruit.

The dancers have all gone under the hill.

Panel Two: Traveler's Reach

At first when you come out of the light, you are relieved. The thunder, the noise in your ears, is over, and the day's surface lies quiet in the yard, bordered with cypress and weeds, wet from the dew. The day lies steadily before you: as in a pond, the negative life of branches and fruit. But this day is not the day you wanted. A common day, being other than this: a well-shaft, with a small disc of light at the bottom—the light of what? Or this: a skating arcade, with lights turning overhead, bouncing underneath the blades, the wheels.

Confined by the day, one day, and the next day, and the body of the day held by a clock, the face of a pond.

And so: the day, the blank street, breaks the blank day, the bald light breaks.

Continues with a bump in the road—to keep you honest and alive, on this side of white—and the day out there, as far as Arizona, or the future, or the mist. Never to see the end of such a day. The day without a day, breaking in the day. And the light without light, only the street. When you come to the end of the street and begin to climb out of the flat, onto the craggy ridges of the heart, when the light is over.

The pre-self comes from the ship, I see him on the gang-plank, grasp his hand, he's come. The day begins when we embrace. I wait for him to come from the road, dust on his arms, the face of the traveler, the man. I am in the photograph, different from it, what it was. I wait for him, as one who falls asleep, the humming-bird standing in hibiscus, the sundial on the grass, and the white chair at ease, under the almond. A mast (mist) on the rim of the sea. The day-ship sailing across the mind, untroubled by water jets of the harbor, a space where the heart lies dumb. A bad learner,.I will never get used to the day, being in it, the word in.

Panel Three: City of Beginning

Beginning is a copy of other cities, at the limits of the earth. It is said that there is a great corral on the outskirts, crowded with every type of animal. Visitors approach from the east and unload their beasts—donkeys, camels, packhorses, elephants, and oxen—and give them to the keeper, before going on foot to the city gates. You take provision for one day's stay, or if you are a trader, goods for a single day in the market. For the city differs from other cities in this: the residents know, have only ever lived, a single day, the last day but one.

Chief exports: linen garments, copper ornamentation for the body, gypsum, various kinds of citrus, and tobacco.

Religion: unknown. Some practice a superstition centered on the day-god, but they write no books, and they have no written creed.

Government: they prefer oligarchy, and hate tyranny.

Pastimes: a festival on the following day, a festival of roasts, when they eat the meat of oxen and chicken and drink a local wine, much beloved of the citizens.

Terrain and climate: from the heights one may glimpse an island shrouded in dreams, where no rain falls. They call it the Other Side of the Day, and it has been a colony of the city *ab initio*, the elders say.

These elders rule the city as benevolent uncles. They seldom sit together in council, going singly about the city to superintend cooking for the festival, which begins at dawn. Young lovers mingle in the fields of sugar cane, the men with trousers tucked into high boots against galliwasps; but the women wear thick hose even the heat of noon. Children have their appointed tasks. They fetch new wood and water from the river. They round up stray animals and deliver them to the corral. All the while they keep one eye on the angle of the sun, and they dream of their own time with a beloved among the grasses, which in some pastures grow taller than the withers of a horse.

Because the end of the city is always around the corner, some of the residents say that their city has no name, or else they believe it was known of old as the City of Unending Nostalgia Tinged with the Certainty of Oblivion. Even the green mountains, they say, and the fields of tobacco, and the groves of citrus, and the leafy mango trees rising from gentle slopes—all seems a memory retained in a photograph after the original has withered, if indeed it ever was, had ever been more than a figment of desire.

Of the colonists on the nearby island, little is known for certain. It is said that they are descended from the men who first voiced these doubts, and over the years others have joined them. The light of the island has the sweet flavor of citrus and rum, and once in it, you become enchanted with the idea of travel, of laying eyes on cities that you find only on the ancient maps. There is no escape from this island, and no defense against it, the eagerness to depart from the known, and come into question.

And so the (un)fortunate mutineers fall asleep, curled up on the grass that borders the shore-line, and caressed by the wind, and blending the lap of the sea with their grunts, they build canoes from oleanders that grow deep in the wood. Their bodies do not age in this artificial island sleep. Birds make their racket from dawn to midnight, and when you move into the bush, you find instead young girls in flowering dresses, singing songs and walking in the clearing, and paying attention to their steps, and their song, but nothing else.

Although on the outside, in the City of Beginning on the mainland, the last day but one will draw to its close, on the island the dreamers escape from the prism of nostalgia, and wander the world like the blacks, traveling in pairs, some to each part of the compass. And as far as we know, they have never stopped more than a night in any of the great marketplaces or ports of the world. For these travelers, the spires of the earth will never be exhausted. But for the young and old in the City of Beginning, the earth will never begin, not offering any more to them than the festival of roasts, or than the cane fields with their beloved; and in the hearts of these people, the day lies heavy like a rock, being the last day but one, the first day.

"There was no day after tomorrow, and no day before that, and no day after yesterday," the elders say, "except the last day, which no one will remember, or understand, being at the limits of our thought."

And so they move toward the limit where ships cannot pass, being in it, and different from it, not knowing anything but the stories that circulate about the travelers on the island, visible from the city, just to the west when you stand at the deep-water port, and then the sun rises, and hits the green forest trees—trees good for the making of their canoes— and also as the sun sets orange in the West, and the water in the harbor goes dark.

Panel Four: the Garden

In the summer of magnificent cities, I was a mule driver and his hefty mule strapped with wine jugs for the city. In the summer of the gardens, I was a bird of plumage displaying my colors to the light—the blazing tongues of hydrogen and oxygen—with the bees in the sunlight, the marigolds red, still swaying in the dust. I went away and came back later to find the camp sacked, and the hill broken, and wreckage. The dead ants floating on a stream from the hose, and the earth dug up from the hill, the flower beds deeply flooded.

Tell me what I can't tell myself
what lies just out of reach of my tongue.

The market-places crowded, pots and pans, ewers, basins, and vases. The festival of roasts. The vases lie unused against the fence. Dust collects on them. The heat causes them to crack. In these vessels I look and look for my favorite word. A simple blue, tinged with yellow, and cracks in a corner, like a web. When the sun sets, the ants grow darker than the earth. They complete their work and return to the hill, climb the sides of earth, and enter the mouth. Ants that circle in a circle that they make. *And if the vessels crack, you do not pour out like water and lose your form.* So forgetful in the mist, all who have come to the river, knelt in the sedge, and had their fill.

Panel Five: A Bird's Portion

The flowers fall, curl up and fall.

No blue petals stain her breast tonight
above the neckline all is confusion
and when she walks in the garden
air escapes like a mouse through a rock—
only solitary creatures can pass her and live
and I am a gardener at best, at worst
a piece of the fence and rusty in the dew
and do not come to her or go like the wind.

And in the garden with the walkers
comes air beating on tiny moth wings
defining a circle and where it cuts
to elude the hands on either side of the arc
her hands and my hands that wander
the gap we know to be intrinsic
a kind of abstract estuary
with grass of its own, and water, and beds
of clematis, and its own wings and dew.

If there was a plan, I must have misplaced it
or swallowed it, and made a new incision
and come out ahead of myself, into the black—
one way to put it, that I came out negative
with too much shock in my system to cope: so

Tell me what I can't tell myself
what lies just out of reach of my tongue
yes? I know more than I know
walking the garden you conjured up last week

walking, eating the ripe melons, coming back from
Genoa to take up my post at the gate
hard to put a finger on just what it is
I want from all these chatterings
some kind of rock to stand on like a lookout
and see the cargoes from Trinidad
the barrels of rum with no slaves dead
and language like a breast, or her, or it, or this

or even the horses, if not the sphere that they cross
or try to and fail, and fall back, and come
back to earth, sweaty from the flight
I am no driver of black stallions from the east
at best, a color looking for a body—
a way to be in your orbit, like the wind

over Linstead by the dam, upon the ledge
at the Pillars of Being—*gallop apace*—
a tree of light flooded with leaves
scattered among the ants, and merely green

And black black black
the black birds clack
in the shak shak tree
—so a poet

opposed to any grain, say, I am not I
some of the ants are flushed in the well
too bright to make them out, each other
anything but the breath they hear in the dark
perpetual movement of an idea

to concur, or the shock, and the walkers in tow
who enter the garden on a Wednesday
to find that the garden has been shut
against their leaving.

Panel Six: Technology

The moth-wings dusted with gold slide across my sight, pinned to a stiff card. The edges of the wing are jagged, a bread knife or some rocks in the shallows. Part one: They enter from the left, move to the center where I catch them, in their transparent body, and move to the right, where they hover in a corner of the retina, and then fade. Part two: The shadows of a wing cross the plantation grass at sunrise, grow larger and darker, and change shape, and openly go into the bright kingdom of the forms, and become white. Both of these accounts have something of the fact of my consternation in them. In front of the shadow left by the wing, the tools grow blunt, uncommunicative, useless—they huddle out of reach of the shape, with me and my friend, and think their way from boredom by advocating bulkier exchanges. We were strolling in the woods when we heard the loud clash of steel, something like cymbals, or a blacksmith, nothing like logic, with its silent couplings, and wedges of despair sprawling down the page, however neat. We found a man there by himself building horse-shoes for a horse standing by the forge, an inconsolable beast with arthritic knees and large bald spots in its coat. The wings were leaves above us, in the sunny air of the common, and language grew elsewhere and green, inviting our bodies to lie down and rest, and to talk to the smith as he worked. "This shoe is for the old horse when he will want to gallop as he did; the time comes round, round like a mango, and then we're back where we started, in the race," the man said. The wings of the horse were folded into his sides. We accepted the cup of water from the smith, and petted the old horse as we spoke to him of our walk, the places we had been. "Everywhere the people are removing," he said. "The people packed up their houses and went that way, two years now, but I had no one to leave with, and so I kept up the smithy, for the horse's sake." He worked obsessively on the shoe as he talked.

Every day the smith opened the stable doors and stoked the fires of his forge, and tied the bucket of peels to the horse's head, and smote the anvil. Wham, Wham. The big hammer rang round us, and we felt the descents like thuds in our chest. Wham, Wham. The horse stumbled with each blow from the hammer and, for the most part, he seemed unsteady on his feet, an old horse begging to be fed and loved. Wham, Wham. It was too hard to bear, to think of the horse like that, and so we talked uneasily for a minute or two, and then said our good-byes to the smith, and we left. The track we'd been on lay on the opposite side of the forge. The thuds followed us back into the wood; gradually, only the brief shudder of the leaves, more sensitive than our ears, told us of the hammer and the wight.

The wings came back as sunlight slanted in the beeches, bright and green, with aromatic shadows now playing on the sedge, in and around the rocks jutting into the earth of our track. We picked our way by and by, stumbling over nothing, only the ghost of the stump was left as the sun went dead, and the wood grew quiet. And then the night birds, the owls and the tree-frogs, the forms of day interrupted. We pitched our camp so as to be ready for the next day's march. And then we slept.

The smith was only a dream I had of felicity with my eyes wide open, walking on the trail. Of his brawn, only the hammer and the sparks, only the smell of dung remains as proof I had seen them at all. And of the hand I was holding, this was in a different section of the forest, far from the blacksmith and his obsession. Sleep within sleep—her sleep and my sleep—doubling the anguish like two mirrors with one person in the middle. And of the two images, both of them are correct, and also in the forest, which complicates matters. One person cannot step onto the trail and greet us. One person is a chimera. Two are necessary for thinking to take place; the dreamer and the one she dreams. Dialogue begins in this.

Panel Seven: Notes for a Book about Danielle

probing through to fever grass in the mist

surprise of finding an empty lot, a broken bicycle, a kid

or people from the mist, a crowd, a field

a sense of wreck to be overcome by a hypothesis

hypothesis about a yard where two stand sufficient, dense

not static—an interchange, a flower

entering and mixing, dying off, resurging, becoming over and over,
with heats and desire of stand

a story—an abstraction from story, of a trip

of desire thwarted, pushing out, but kept in, kept away from the
conditions of its lot

A spume that plays upon the ghostly paradigm of things

bodies of the cave, the light projects shadows of other bodies on the
window of the skull

a teaser of desire to become form, a flash within the minutiae of syn-
tax, sealed mouths open

common light, daylight to the white, to the colorless, to the bright
light

but before this light

golden-thighed one, Pythagoras

and a story to tell, with everything that causes it, from where they come to a fork, and then separate, like air from lungs

a wind of monstrosity—*break break break*

cold stones, the sea

The reservoir as a cliff. A massive problem of logistics to get it right. Smooth sides for all of that. A circle.

And the blazing heat if you stand in one place, a dangerous solitude, and irreversible.

Sister to the bigger basin where the shore coughs up froth. Jagged teeth of the moon on sea, of the coast.

"I can't stand it. Please explain to me why you did that. How much gasoline to the next motel?"

The axiomatic or atomic fury of the clouds and our terror. How it crashes in over my head.

The blaze of the guns. Trenches down your front. We should have been born before the sky went dead and the hullabaloo took away our nerve.

In short, we were happier than we deserved, but only for a while. The circles of light will outlast the dialectic of the good, the rivers of light. (The light.)

Panel Eight: Interlude

You require some explanation. You think, perhaps, it was not right to
tell it like that, the sentences so depleted of juice. It was nine months
ago. A delphic nightingale sits in the branches of the forest at Dodona,
and this is what it says. *Circles pricked through with cones, and the seed of
perishing also the seed of light.* How else could it be? I had washed up on
the sand, outside the taxonomy of the biologists—outside the possibil-
ities of syntax to express. I was a beast, the enemy of birds. The way one
fine morning you're asked to pretend you're a snake, and everyone gets
down on his stomach and slithers and gets dirty. Some ridiculous change
had overtaken my life. I stopped going out of the house for any reason.
I lay quiet on the floor, day after day, eating slices of bread and nothing
much else. I ignored the telephone, the heaps of mail, and the knocks
on my door at all hours. Things could have gone on like this, indefi-
nitely, except that one day, I looked up and saw that the weather had
turned bleak. The trees had started to shed.

Let me tell you more closely how it was. From time to time, random
images erupted like hallucinations and I caught myself helpless before a
kind of video screen. But this screen was projected from within, onto
the back of my skull. I saw us creep toward a pear tree and make off with
fruit that belonged to another man. And I heard the word again as I
spoke it, well-chosen for its point, that broke the rules of decency and
stabbed her in the back, and drove her to weep and from the restaurant.
And other events. But whatever the picture, it told the same story, it was
meant only for me. And yet, none of these terrible sequences demand-
ed my suicide. For before that juncture, a thousand years were to pass
on the Meadow of Wailing, a thousand years until we moved toward a
cleft in the rocks that stood in the east, cleansed and lighter than the
dust, on our final journey. But I am getting ahead of myself. On the sec-
ond day in the Valley the symptoms intensified. We all thought we were
going to collapse from boredom and regret, but we knew deep down
that no, it wasn't like that. The tongue grows heavy like a slab of metal,
impossible to move, and with your body racked by moans, you're try-
ing hard to catch a breath. When you do manage to take in some air,

you find that it's rancid. Plus, I was struggling to keep from touching the heart next to mine—which would have doubled our sorrow—at the very moment I was most in need of contact with bodies. But there were no bodies, only a heap of discarded clothing on the plain. I had been expelled from the recurrent nightmare of egoism. I had become, in the words of a poet, "a dull slave grinding at a heavy quern"—and a man without conviction or friends, and no real plan. In the end, I had reverted to my phenotype. The answer had been in front of my face all along. But what then?

· · · ·

One morning I went out into the snow and put some of it in my pockets. I put it in my shirt, underneath my sweater, and stuck my foot in a drift up to my shins. I then covered my head with the snow, and like that, with my hair gone to white, I stood by the bird-bath, I don't know, waiting for the spring. I ignored the scuffles of my body, the fight I was in. A few winter birds—they were twits, I think—had been left behind in the trees, and you know how loud they can get. The birds were restless, jumping from branch to branch, leaving the maples to regroup in the hedges, and flying back and forth to the bird-bath in the open space. The sky was clearing up as the afternoon went along. The sky was closed now for good. I was starting to shiver, but then one by one, the old self and the dead self climbed from the pit with Danielle and stood up in front of me. We were two people out of our heads. Perhaps it was the influence of something I had read that winter, a seductive nihilism—but even that would have been understandable. To have been under an illusion about the Mythos, and now clarified. There's no difference, I said to her. Where had everyone gone to? The noises had died down in the garden. The fighting had stopped, and I went with the flow. *Like a long-legged fly upon the stream.* It's funny to think about it now, to go over it. Talking to myself in the plural, everyone solemn but pleased at some remarkable turn of events. We had lost our nerve; we had all choked, as the expression went. But they were no help to me, that day out in the snow, no help at all.

The upshot of all this stupidity is that I caught pneumonia and couldn't get out of bed for over two months. And that's how I confronted the spring of 19____, flat on my back, mumbling in and out of delirium, noticing that the blossoms had arrived but not remembering when, and feeling the days lengthen around me but not aware of how much time had elapsed. I was elsewhere; I was in two places at once—or was it that one place had become two? I was in bed, and no longer like myself, underneath the surfaces of a pond with tiny one-celled animals floating and multiplying. It was vague, where the animals lived. I hadn't gone very far, but there was a suggestion of terror and also a kind of immunity from it, if only my body would relax below the pond, and keep its eyes and ears opened. If I turned to look elsewhere, then a powerful anxiety would start up—the Greek article *ai*, in the feminine plural, expanded and filled in the foreground of what I saw; and occupying the dark mud in the heart of it, the seed of perishing like a mouth, dark dark   dark, everything around it was dark, and no ground to stand on and fight.

All of this was part of my delirium. Some of it no doubt came from the books I had read or the television, maybe the bulk of it did. But during this time, I crossed paths with no agreeable images—no cornucopia; no swimming or dozing at the beach, in the shade of an almond; no victory dances or festivals of the Jonkanoo—nothing of the kind to stimulate delight—for I experienced no lovemaking with a big-hipped woman, no apotheosis of the national hero, no flowering poinsettia trees on the slope, in the botanical gardens.

I had entered the paintings of Max Ernst and Wifredo Lam and become nothing more than a shape of shapes: a round demon fading into the canvas like old paint, no longer visible and distinct, or clear and distinct like an idea, not a vermilion feather from a parrot, and not much more than an outline.

I don't know. How much of what I saw happening was in the dream, and how much belonged to the other dreamers, to the elders? How much of what I knew and was had been passed on to me?

The languages scrolled in front of my face from top to bottom, poem after poem of unintelligible sentences and confused punctuation, and in the silence of these words the bull, the forms of hardship spreading from Niger to the shores of the Congo, northward to the Delta, and then west again, to the point of Cadmus's embarkation. I said to the poet of the sentences:

Tell me what I can't tell myself
what lies just out of reach of my tongue.

The city of your speech was before my time, and will be standing still after my time is over. This much I know: what I cannot hope to know. I know only this: that before the sun stopped its whistle in the stony legs of Memnon, which told us of the dawn's approach; and before the pale blue fires of hell began to spit, and the gates of delivery were shut—that before these events took place, your poetry was already a hard dwelling upon the earth, the result of migrations long ago. And yet, between the time of its making and my discovery of it, this time is as nothing next to the time to follow—and when I look at it like this, I can't stand it, the city begins to seem fragile and not ancient, but only a transitory idea, and desperately brief, like a drop of water on a hot-plate. I hate the thought of this death. Then it was over, and I was well enough to sit with a book in my lap, and to look out at the garden, and even to go outside for a walk, on the warmer days.

In those weeks of my convalescence, the afternoon light hit upon the apples with a breathtaking clarity. My front room was like a chamber flooded with light, tangible, irreducible, and strong; things shifted in it, and acquired a glow, a capacity of depth and thingness, and a color. It was the light as light, stripped of metaphor, something produced by the sun and reaching through the window like a messenger, and the message was—itself. Here I am, the light said. You can talk all you want, but this is how it's going to be. I won't make you rich, and I can't bring back the months you lost, and I won't sweet-talk a girl into your bed. You poets are always asking the light for hand-outs like that. I don't want your incense, or any bulls. Nonetheless, here I am, *poikilothron'*, to be with you for a little while, as long as it lasts. With this language pouring in at the window, I felt calm for the first time in months, more possible or even plausible as a self—.

I had visited several cities during this time, and now I could say what they had been: only camels on the horizon of a song, and it took them a whole year to make the crossing. A caravan of cities, each of them with its own courtyard, fountains, and sculpture. These were the cities of my imagination. One day, when I looked up from my book, they had gone.

~ Morningside Memoirs

:

Observe, as the philosopher writes, *the sun warm and luminous in every direction, and the immortal bodies drenched in its violet radiance.* Someone reads this sentence and then wanders off to drink hot stout on the concrete steps of St. John the Divine cathedral. This someone is me.

One evening, someone sat here with a pot of ale to think about the myth of the horses and the charioteer. Many things occur only once in the life of the universe. Pot of ale, pint of stout—the taste of each. (Sexual desire as the violent separation of light into spectra: shifted towards the red, the black part of the tongue.)

Observe, nonetheless, the immortal bodies imprisoned in the sentence of the philosopher—that sun, how real it seems! that radiance, don't you feel the warmth on your neck?

I am the first. No one has sat on the steps of this cathedral, with a pint of stout, to whisper the phrases of Herakleitos. But let me be more precise: no Jamaican has done this. I am the only poet to sit on these steps, in daylight or twilight, to whisper the Greek spoken by the horses of Achilles.

Nonetheless, observe the undying manes, the leathery sides bulging: the weeping of the animals for the death of Achilles' lover. How real they seem!

An older poet sitting on these steps would see things differently: the rapid motion of the coaches, the horses in descent to the Battery or Bowery, a long line of motion to the shattered legs in the cane fields at Madeira. To the wailing of women, to the wailing of souls in the cargo holds.

Observe, nonetheless, the mortal bodies drenched by the afternoon's sun, with the fountain next door sending out signals of a fine mist. No matter.

I am the Negro under the architrave. I am the only Jamaican in this blasted century to whisper the language of the horses that weep. (On these cathedral steps.) No matter the logic of the bodies drenched from the fountain's signals. Only these bodies are real. Only this pot of ale. This sun.

~ Spring Journal

.

To say it all at once: past the row of hibiscus, the untended ground of the open land in front of the gully. Once inside this area, trousers tied at the cuff because of scorpions and beetles amid the long weeds, return to the clipped lawn was hazardous. The excitement of an outbound trip counters the fear of what lies to either side of the highway, just underfoot as it were, and this explains how only in the midst of junk, thick fever grass hiding holes, vermin, sharp rusty sheet iron, etc., did thought of hazard reach up and pinch our nerves. The gully itself, a graveyard for upcountry refuse—caravels of zinc and wood, tree limbs like torsos, old crates—in truth was no more than a widening gash at the outer limit of the property. The chasm grew more precipitous with each arrival of the rainy season until the footholds disappeared and the open land shrank. What made it family, also made it dangerous, because though one could slide to the bottom intact, getting back out again was slippery business. The engineers came and filled in the eroded parts. They put up stone walls and paved the ground to improve drainage. Henceforth, things flowed, edges had been defined. It was safe to go out once the rains had stopped, to inspect the damage and to pay one's respects to them. (The hero's head sang even then of his love.)

Looking over the gully to the asphalt on the far side where the busses make slow passage full to the top, with market produce and tins, animals in cages, meant for the market at Cross Roads. Saturdays again found them squeezing pears and choosing yams from the crocus-bag tarpaulins spread before the stalls. Nor at this juncture, with its own point of view, could Danielle occupy the Claremont apartment, since only one episode, and this one alone, can come forward at a pop. The blue curtains have not yet been sewn by Tanya; the toy motorcyclist, a clown's head and grimace, has not yet arrived from the West Coast. The amusing ornament collected by Danielle—such as, but they have disappeared—I climbed into her bed with my winter coat on. Earlier that evening: Charles gesturing in the living room (where the curtains hang) to make his point unmistakable; two French women French kissing after M*A*S*H; Tanya's brown quilt and Tanya herself, foggy, boulder-shaped, and evil, countering the point. And even earlier: how rocks thrown across the channel fled through the bus windows lumbering up Old Hope Road; how pebbles from a sling-shot dug up the earth just short of ground doves (stupid, common). Bigger game, such as white wings and pea doves, nested up higher, and drew the boys to the foot of the hill, where bramble and stories begin. (Indifference to long nail-sharp spikes did not of course guarantee that one returned with a pullet.) White wings and pea doves were the first real prize we had.

One sees Norsemen through pages of type as if through serial horizons, they multiply up and down, they cut across the line of sight. Similarly, names come back charred upon the spits of things. Customs were picked up overseas, assimilated, and applied to the vernacular. A noh musik dat. There were the girls: Michelle who had a small face, and Elaine, a smaller version of Danielle, and Sandra whose height grew to be more than her age, and Grace. And there were the teachers, pock-marked and smelly, brown as the grass, the uniforms that the boys wore, plump tamarinds from a limb before a stone cracks into them. They break and jerk loose; and they fall to the floor of the common. Division takes place in the schoolroom and on the playing field. The parting from the womb stayed with them like a congenital tear in the eye, that growing up could succor and did not.

Turning to one cameo, several cameos jump forward demanding to be heard. Like monitoring a roomful of oscilloscopes against the cessation of the blip, one cannot play favorites and survive. Peels of reference, chips in a wash, in a catalogue of drift. A white powder settles. Contours of events—no detail anymore—alone tell that she and I took the cliff walk at Newport. Horizontal not deep moments, a transformation of three dimensions into two. Wires connect the arms to several bells and to reach forward rings them arbitrarily. The tablecloth hides each piece of furniture secure in chaotic play.

The floors back then had just been redone and the piano stood in the bright light of the bay window, where her bed stands now. People with and without names watched the television. Girls became women, boys became. Everyone got married and moved to farms and gave birth to twins. The motorcycle is still tied to the fence above the trash dump but the girl herself, and her professional camera, grew apart from everyone and left. She might have crossed the Hudson river later in life, to get at the cheaper rents. But then again.

~ Au Café Noir

The piano's bone white oars are pressed
to music of falling water. Her passions
clink softly in the courtyard, and a Venus
entering the bath, rocks gently on his notes.
The waves fall from her rough shoulders.

A blush of body rises on sleeping trees.
Caught in the tide, they sway to the brink
walk over leafy rivers to the white basin.
Their own foot soles are the rocks: a bridge
of notes like ear rings on a tinted stream.

Coracle bears the acolyte and his mistress
in tremor of arms, off from the recital.
Camisoles, a residue of decomposing bars,
bloom in the centre: *Mater saeva Cupidinum*,
hidden among the rocks of Leonardo's genius.

Toward morning, the brush is put in water.
A peep from the radiator: then choirs rise
flutter in the yard and stevedores begin
unpacking heads, sweeping away the litter.
The iron chairs arrange themselves at table

and nymphs come down from the pediment.
Summer over the yard went with the tide.
Flutes are put up, the piano is a ship
but no paddle or slaves to work the bones.
I drink café noir to buck up the sunrise.

ROOF BOOKS

- Andrews, Bruce. **EX WHY ZEE**. 112p. $10.95.
- Andrews, Bruce. **Getting Ready To Have Been Frightened**. 116p. $7.50.
- Benson, Steve. **Blue Book**. Copub. with The Figures. 250p. $12.50
- Bernstein, Charles. **Islets/Irritations**. 112p. $9.95.
- Bernstein, Charles (editor). **The Politics of Poetic Form**. 246p. $12.95; cloth $21.95.
- Brossard, Nicole. **Picture Theory**. 188p. $11.95.
- Cadiot, Olivier. **Former, Future, Fugitive**. Translated by Cole Swensen. 166p. $13.95.
- Champion, Miles. **Three Bell Zero**. 72p. $10.95.
- Child, Abigail. **Scatter Matrix**. 79p. $9.95.
- Davies, Alan. **Active 24 Hours**. 100p. $5.
- Davies, Alan. **Signage**. 184p. $11.
- Davies, Alan. **Rave**. 64p. $7.95.
- Day, Jean. **A Young Recruit**. 58p. $6.
- Di Palma, Ray. **Motion of the Cypher**. 112p. $10.95.
- Di Palma, Ray. **Raik**. 100p. $9.95.
- Doris, Stacy. **Kildare**. 104p. $9.95.
- Dreyer, Lynne. **The White Museum**. 80p. $6.
- Edwards, Ken. **Good Science**. 80p. $9.95.
- Eigner, Larry. **Areas Lights Heights**. 182p. $12, $22 (cloth).
- Gizzi, Michael. **Continental Harmonies**. 92p. $8.95.
- Goldman, Judith. **Vocoder**. 96p. $11.95.
- Gottlieb, Michael. **Ninety-Six Tears**. 88p. $5.
- Gottlieb, Michael. **Gorgeous Plunge**. 96p. $11.95.
- Gottlieb, Michael. **Lost & Found**. 80p. $11.95.
- Greenwald, Ted. **Jumping the Line**. 120p. $12.95.
- Grenier, Robert. **A Day at the Beach**. 80p. $6.
- Grosman, Ernesto. **The XULReader: An Anthology of Argentine Poetry (1981–1996)**. 167p. $14.95.
- Guest, Barbara. **Dürer in the Window, Reflexions on Art**. Book design by Richard Tuttle. Four color throughout. 80p. $24.95.
- Hills, Henry. **Making Money**. 72p. $7.50. VHS videotape $24.95. Book & tape $29.95.
- Huang Yunte. **SHI: A Radical Reading of Chinese Poetry**. 76p. $9.95
- Hunt, Erica. **Local History**. 80 p. $9.95.
- Kuszai, Joel (editor) **poetics@**, 192 p. $13.95.
- Inman, P. **Criss Cross**. 64 p. $7.95.
- Inman, P. **Red Shift**. 64p. $6.
- Lazer, Hank. **Doublespace**. 192 p. $12.
- Lazer, Hank. **Doublespace**. 192 p. $12.
- Levy, Andrew. **Paper Head Last Lyrics**. 112 p. $11.95.
- Mac Low, Jackson. **Representative Works: 1938–1985**. 360p. $12.95, $18.95 (cloth).

- Mac Low, Jackson. **Twenties**. 112p. $8.95.
- Moriarty, Laura. **Rondeaux**. 107p. $8.
- Neilson, Melanie. **Civil Noir**. 96p. $8.95.
- Pearson, Ted. **Planetary Gear**. 72p. $8.95.
- Perelman, Bob. **Virtual Reality**. 80p. $9.95.
- Perelman, Bob. **The Future of Memory**. 120p. $14.95.
- Piombino, Nick, **The Boundary of Blur**. 128p. $13.95.
- Raworth, Tom. **Clean & Will-Lit**. 106p. $10.95.
- Robinson, Kit. **Balance Sheet**. 112p. $11.95.
- Robinson, Kit. **Democracy Boulevard**. 104p. $9.95.
- Robinson, Kit. **Ice Cubes**. 96p. $6.
- Scalapino, Leslie. **Objects in the Terrifying Tense Longing from Taking Place**. 88p. $9.95.
- Seaton, Peter. **The Son Master**. 64p. $5.
- Sherry, James. **Popular Fiction**. 84p. $6.
- Silliman, Ron. **The New Sentence**. 200p. $10.
- Silliman, Ron. **N/O**. 112p. $10.95.
- Smith, Rod. **Music or Honesty**. 96p. $12.95
- Smith, Rod. **Protective Immediacy**. 96p. $9.95
- Stefans, Brian Kim. **Free Space Comix**.
- Tarkos, Christophe. **Ma Langue est Poétique—Selected Works**. 96p. $12.95.
- Templeton, Fiona. **Cells of Release**. 128p. with photographs. $13.95.
- Templeton, Fiona. **YOU—The City**. 150p. $11.95.
- Torres, Edwin. **The All-Union Day of the Shock Worker**. 112 p. $10.95.
- Ward, Diane. **Human Ceiling**. 80p. $8.95.
- Ward, Diane. **Relation**. 64p. $7.50.
- Watson, Craig. **Free Will**. 80p. $9.95.
- Watten, Barrett. **Progress**. 122p. $7.50.
- Weiner, Hannah. **We Speak Silent**. 76 p. $9.95
- Wolsak, Lissa. **Pen Chants**. 80p. $9.95.
- Yasusada, Araki. **Doubled Flowering: From the Notebooks of Araki Yasusada**. 272p. $14.95.

ROOF BOOKS
are published by
Segue Foundation, 303 East 8th Street, New York, NY 10009
Visit our website at **segue.org**

ROOF BOOKS are distributed by
SMALL PRESS DISTRIBUTION
1341 Seventh Avenue, Berkeley, CA. 94710-1403.
Phone orders: 800-869-7553
spdbooks.org